Dutch
cooking today

KOSMOS

Kosmos Uitgevers, Utrecht/Antwerpen

Contents

Breakfast, brunch and lunch 7

Cakes with tea or coffee 21

Appetizers and snacks 29

Soups 39

Mashed dishes (stamppotten) and other one-pan dishes 55

Main courses 75

Vegetables and side dishes 97

Desserts 107

Index 124

Breakfast, brunch and lunch

Poffertjes: Tiny Cheese Pancakes with Herb Butter

serves 4 | preparation: approx. 25 min

400 ml / 14 fl oz milk
15 g / ½ oz fresh yeast or
7 g / ½ teaspoon dried yeast
200 g / 7 oz flour
100 g / 3½ oz buckwheat flour
pinch of salt
1 egg
100 g / 3½ oz mature Gouda
or other full-flavoured cheese
freshly ground pepper
40 g /1½ oz melted butter
For the herb butter:
125 g / 4 oz softened butter
1 tablespoon lemon juice
1 teaspoon finely chopped parsley
1 teaspoon finely chopped chives
1 teaspoon finely chopped chervil

- For the herb butter combine the butter, lemon juice and finely chopped herbs in a bowl. Set aside.

- Warm the milk until lukewarm. Crumble or sprinkle the yeast into a small bowl, add a splash of milk and mix until smooth. In a bowl, beat the flour, buckwheat flour, salt, yeast mixture, egg and the remaining warm milk with a whisk to a smooth batter. Whisk to remove any lumps. Cover and leave to rise for 1 hour in a warm place.

- Stir the grated cheese and pepper into the batter. Lightly grease the 'poffertjes' pan and fill the depressions about half full with the batter. Quickly fry the tiny pancakes. Turn them when golden and almost dry and fry the other side.

- Serve with a knob of herb butter.

Delicious with halved cherry tomatoes.

For this recipe you need a traditional 'poffertjes' pan or else you must increase the milk to 3/4 litre and fry small pancakes with 1-2 tablespoons of batter.

Brabant Sausage Rolls

makes 8 | preparation: approx. 30 min | rising: 25 min | oven: 20 min

½ packet white bread mix
50 g / 2 oz softened butter
150 ml / 5 fl oz lukewarm water
salt
Filling:
1 egg
2 cloves garlic
200 g / 7 oz minced beef and pork
2 tablespoons fine breadcrumbs
salt and freshly ground pepper
2 tablespoons finely chopped mixed herbs (thyme, parsley and oregano)
flour for dusting
poppy seeds

- In a bowl, combine the bread mix with the butter, water and a pinch of salt. Knead thoroughly until smooth and elastic. Cover with a tea towel and leave to rise for 25 minutes in a warm place.

- Make the filling. In a small bowl, beat the egg. Put 2 tablespoons aside for brushing the rolls later. Peel and finely chop the garlic. In a bowl combine the mince with the beaten egg, garlic, bread-crumbs, salt, pepper and herbs.

- Roll the mince to 8 sausage shapes, each about 10 cm (4 in) long. Roll the sausages in the flour.

- Heat the oven to 200°C / 400°F.

- On a lightly floured work surface, roll the dough into an oblong shape and cut into 8 pieces, each 10 x 15 cm (4 x 6 in). Moisten the edges of the dough and place a sausage on each piece of dough. Fold the dough over and firmly seal the edges. Brush the sausage rolls with the remaining egg and sprinkle with poppy seeds. Place on a lined baking tray and bake for about 20 minutes until golden brown and cooked.

Wentelteefjes: French Toast with Lemon

serves 4 | preparation: approx. 15 min

1 egg
grated rind of 1 lemon or
2 teaspoons ground cinnamon
150 ml / 5 fl oz milk
4 slices stale white bread
30 g / 1oz butter
2 tablespoons soft, brown sugar

- In a bowl, beat the egg and stir in the lemon peel or cinnamon and milk. Remove the crusts from the bread.

- Dip the slices of bread in the egg mixture. Next put the slices on top of each other in the bowl so that they absorb all the remaining liquid.
In a large frying pan, heat the butter over a moderate heat. Fry the bread on both sides until golden brown.

- Serve the French toast sprinkled with soft brown sugar.

Three-in-a-Pan with Orange and Cinnamon Sugar

serves 4 | preparation: approx. 25 min

200 g / 7 oz self-raising flour
salt
1 egg
200 ml / 7 fl oz milk
juice and grated zest of 1 orange
2 teaspoons cinnamon
100 g / 3½ oz sugar
30 g / 1 oz butter

- Sieve the flour with a pinch of salt into a bowl. Add the egg and half the milk and mix to a smooth batter. Stirring continuously, add the remaining milk to make a thin batter. Stir in the orange juice and grated zest.

- In a small bowl, combine the cinnamon and sugar.

- Heat a little butter in a frying pan and add three heaping spoonfuls of batter. Cook the three-in-a-pan over moderate heat until light brown, then turn and cook the other side until golden brown. Repeat the process with the remaining batter. Keep the pancakes warm.

- Serve with cinnamon sugar.

Delicious with a spoonful of marmalade.

Tomatoes Stuffed with Egg Salad

serves 4 | preparation: approx. 20 min

4 canned anchovy fillets , drained
3 tablespoons milk
4 medium tomatoes
4 hard-boiled eggs
100 ml / 3½ oz crème fraîche
50 ml / 2 fl oz mayonnaise
freshly ground pepper
2 tablespoons finely chopped chives + extra to garnish
1 tablespoon drained capers or black imitation caviar

• Soak the anchovy fillets for 10 minutes in the milk. Slice the tops off the tomatoes and carefully hollow out with a spoon or grapefruit knife. Turn upside down on paper towel to drain. Remove the anchovy fillets from the milk and pat them dry with paper towel.

• Peel the eggs and chop them with the anchovy fillets into small pieces. Stir in the crème fraîche, mayonnaise, pepper and chives.

• Stuff the tomatoes with the egg salad and garnish with chives, capers or caviar. Arrange on a serving dish and serve.

Delicious with warm toast.

Uitsmijter: Fried Eggs with Raw Ham and Mustard Cheese

serves 4 | preparation: approx. 10 min

25 g / 1 oz butter + butter for the bread
4 eggs
4 slices Dutch mustard cheese (or mustard Cheddar)
salt and freshly ground pepper
4 slices wholemeal farmhouse bread
100 g / 3 ½ oz sliced raw ham
4 gherkins, sliced into 'fans'
2 tomatoes, quartered
finely chopped parsley

• In a large frying pan, melt the butter. Break the eggs into the pan and fry for a few minutes on a low heat.

• Arrange a slice of mustard cheese around each yolk and season to taste. Cover the pan and cook the eggs a few minutes more until done and the cheese has melted.

• Toast the slices of bread and spread with butter. Top with ham and place a fried egg on top. Garnish with gherkin, tomato and parsley.

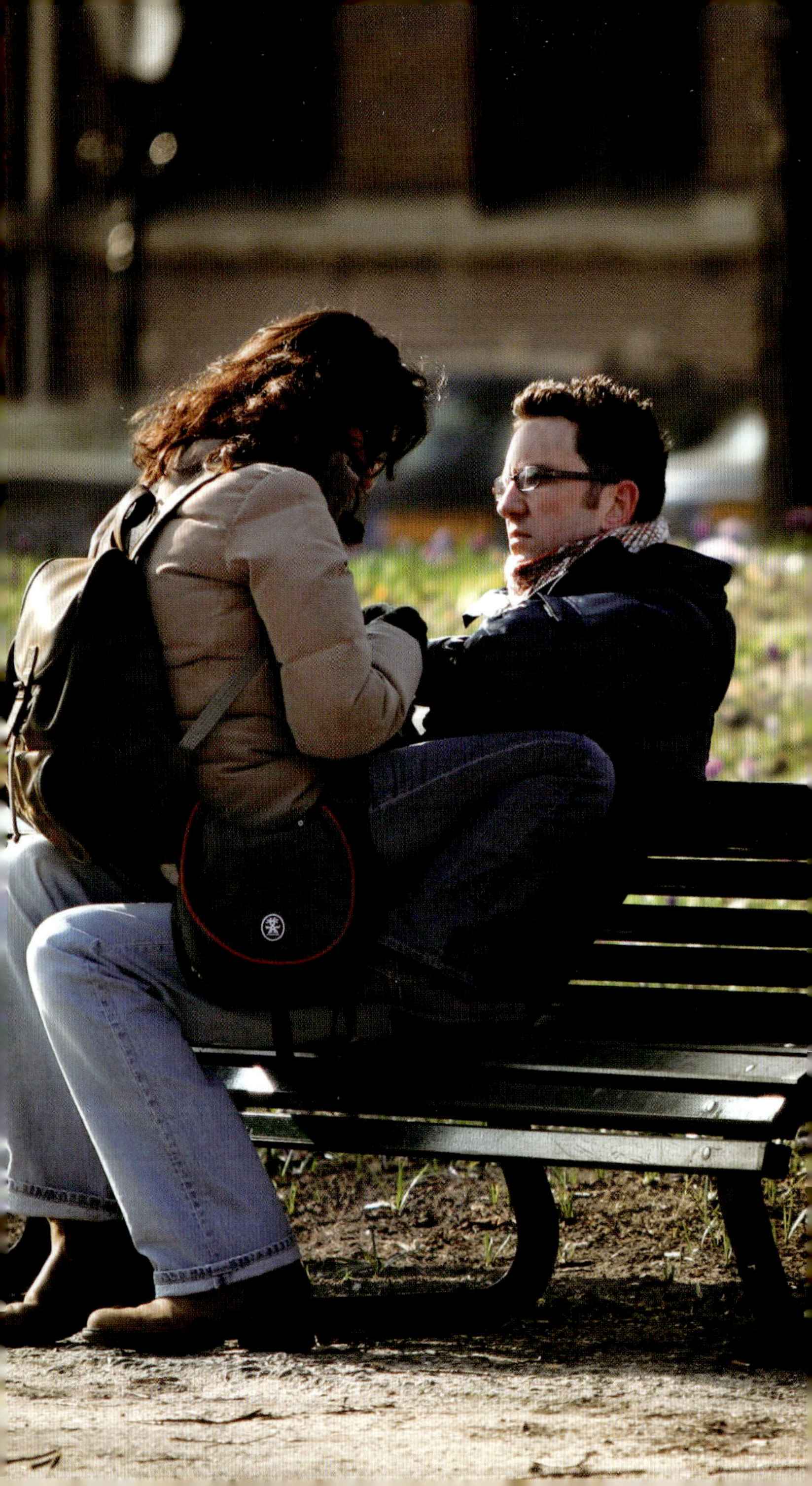

Cakes with tea or coffee

Butter Cake with Apricot Filling

approx. 10 wedges | preparation: approx. 15 min | oven: 15-20 min

250 g / 8 oz flour
175 g / 6 oz white caster sugar
salt
225 g / 7 oz cold butter
100 g / 3½ oz soaked dried apricots
50 g / 2 oz flaked almonds
2 tablespoons ginger syrup
1 tablespoon milk

- Preheat the oven to 200°C / 400°F.

- In a bowl combine the flour, sugar and a pinch of salt. Cut the butter into pieces and mix into the flour. Then, using a pastry cutter or two knives, cut the butter into fine pieces. With cool hands, knead the butter and flour together and gather up into a firm dough ball. You can also easily make the dough in a food processor.

- Finely chop the apricots and mix them with the almonds and ginger syrup.

- Grease a 24 cm / 10 in round cake dish with butter. Press half the dough into the dish. Spread the apricot mixture over the top. Roll out the other half of the dough on a lightly floured work surface to the same size as the dish. Place over the filling and press the edges together.

- Using the blunt side of a knife, score a crisscross pattern on the top and brush with milk. Bake the butter cake in the oven for 15-20 minutes until cooked and golden brown.

- Allow to cool and slice the cake into wedges just before serving.

Dutch Apple Pie

approx. 10 wedges | preparation: approx. 30 min | oven: 45 min

- 300 g / 10 oz flour + extra
- 125 g / 4 oz white caster sugar
- salt
- 200 g / 7 oz chilled butter + extra
- 1 egg yolk
- 100 g / 3½ oz raisins
- 100 ml / 3½ fl oz orange juice
- 1 kg / 2 lb firm apples (Elstar, Jona Gold, peeled and sliced)
- 2 tablespoons custard powder
- 2 teaspoons cinnamon
- 2 tablespoons sugar
- 3 tablespoons apricot jam

● In a bowl, combine the flour, sugar and a pinch of salt. Dice the butter and mix into the flour. Use a pastry cutter or two knives to cut the butter into small pieces. Add the egg yolk and knead everything together with cool hands. Roll into a firm ball. Grease a 24 cm / 10 in cake tin with a removable bottom with butter and press 2/3 of the dough over the bottom and sides. Refrigerate the tin and remaining dough until ready to use.

● Preheat the oven to 175°C / 375°F. Put the raisins and orange juice in a pan, bring to a boil and simmer until the liquid has evaporated, about 5 minutes.

● Combine the apple, raisins, custard powder, cinnamon and sugar. Spread over the pastry base. Roll out the rest of the pastry and cut into 1 cm / 1/2 in strips. Arrange in a crisscross pattern on top of the apple mixture, pressing the pastry edges together.

● Bake the apple pie about 45 minutes in the oven until golden brown. Remove from the oven and glaze with apricot jam. Allow to cool in the cake tin for 10 minutes. Remove from the tin and serve.

Speculaas: Spiced Biscuit

5 biscuits | preparation: approx. 45 min | resting: 2 hours to 1 day | oven: 30 min

200 g / 7 oz self-raising cake flour
125 g / 4 oz soft brown sugar
2 tablespoons mixed spice
pinch salt
150 g / 5 oz chilled butter
1 tablespoon milk

• In a bowl combine the cake flour, brown sugar, mixed spice and a pinch of salt. Dice the butter and mix into the flour. Then using a pastry cutter or two knives cut through the flour into smaller pieces. Add the milk and with cool hands quickly knead everything to a firm dough.

• Wrap the dough in clingfilm and leave to rest in a cool place for at least 2 hours, but preferably for a day to develop the spice flavour.

• Preheat the oven to 175°C / 375°F. Roll out the dough into a rectangle about 1 cm / 1/2 in thick. Place this (or two smaller rectangles) on a lined baking tray and bake the spiced biscuit in the oven for about 30 minutes until done.

• Cool the biscuit on a wire rack. Break the biscuit in pieces and serve.

Appetizers and snacks

Smoked Eel Appetizers

makes 12 | preparation: approx. 10 min

1 lemon
50 g / 2 oz softened butter
2 tablespoons finely chopped chives
salt and freshly ground pepper
3 slices white bread
100 g / 3 ½ oz smoked eel, at room temperature

- Halve the lemon. Slice one half in 3 slices and cut each slice into quarters. Grate the peel of the other half lemon. In a bowl combine the grated peel, butter, chives, a few drops lemon juice and salt and pepper to taste.

- Toast the bread and quarter each slice. Cut the smoked eel into 12 equal pieces.

- Spread the chive butter onto the toast and place a piece of smoked eel on each square. Garnish with lemon and serve.

Herring in Mustard Cream Appetizers

makes 12 | preparation: approx. 10 min

125 ml crème fraîche
1 teaspoon mustard
2 spring onions, finely chopped
2 salted herrings, cut in strips
salt and freshly ground pepper
12 small toasts or small rounds or pumpernickel
½ red onion, chopped very finely

- In a bowl, combine the crème fraîche, mustard and half the spring onions. Mix in the herring and season to taste.

- Spread the herring in mustard cream on the toasts or rounds of pumpernickel and garnish with red onion and the remaining spring onions. Arrange the herring appetizers on a platter and serve.

Cheese Puffs

makes 4 | preparation: approx. 25 min | oven: 20 min

40 g / 1 ½ oz butter
½ teaspoon curry powder
25 g / 1 oz flour
200 ml / 7 fl oz milk
100 g / 3 ½ oz mature Gouda or Cheddar cheese, grated
8 sheets ready-made frozen puff pastry, thawed
1 tomato, skinned, seeded, cubed and patted dry
2 spring onions, thinly sliced
25 g / 1 oz grated mature Gouda cheese and / or Parmesan cheese
2 tablespoons sesame seeds

- Preheat the oven to 200°C / 400°F.

- In a saucepan, melt 25 g / 1 oz butter and briefly fry the curry powder. Mix in the flour and gradually stir in the milk. Continue stirring until the sauce thickens and simmer gently for another 5 minutes. Remove the pan from the heat and add the grated cheese. Leave to cool.

- Stir the tomato and spring onions into the cheese sauce. Cut each pastry sheet in two and make an incision every centimetre (or half inch) along half of the halved sheets. Spread the cheese mixture over the other half of the sheets to within 1 cm / 1/2 in of the pastry edge. Melt the remaining butter and brush the pastry edges. Place the incised pastry sheets on top and firmly press the edges together.

- Place the cheese puffs on a lined baking tray and brush with melted butter. Sprinkle with grated cheese and/or sesame seeds.

- Bake in the middle of the oven for 20 minutes until golden brown.

Bitterballen: Bite-Size Croquettes

makes 24 | preparation: approx. 1½ hours | cooling: 2 hours

200 g / 7 oz stewing beef or veal, cubed
1 bouquet garni
400 ml / 14 fl oz beef stock (from 1 stock cube)
30 g / 1 oz butter
30 g / 1 oz flour
salt and freshly ground pepper
nutmeg
vegetable oil for deep-frying
2 eggs
100 g / 3½ oz fine, dry breadcrumbs

- In a pan, bring the meat, bouquet garni and beef stock slowly to the boil. Simmer on a low heat for about 1 hour until the meat is tender. Strain off 200 ml / 7 fl oz stock into a measuring jug. Chop the cooked meat very finely.

- In a pan, melt the butter and stir in the flour. Still stirring, add the stock and continue stirring until the sauce is thick and smooth. Leave the sauce to cook gently for about 2 minutes. Stir in the meat and add salt, pepper and nutmeg to taste. Pour the ragout onto a flat plate, cool and refrigerate 2 hours until firm.

- Heat oil in a deep frying pan to 180°C / 350°F. In a shallow bowl, beat the eggs with one tablespoon of water. Put the breadcrumbs in a shallow bowl. Shape the ragout into 24 balls and roll in the breadcrumbs. Then roll in the beaten egg and breadcrumbs again.

- Deep-fry the croquettes 6 at a time for 3-4 minutes until brown and crisp. Drain on paper towels. Arrange the bite-size croquettes on a serving dish and serve with coarse mustard.

Zebras

makes 16 | preparation: approx. 10 min | chilling: 1 hour

100 g / 3 ½ oz softened butter
200 g / 7 oz cream cheese
100 g / 3 ½ oz smoked salmon, finely chopped
1 tablespoon finely chopped fresh dill
salt and freshly ground pepper
8 slices rye bread or pumpernickel

- With a mixer, beat the butter and cream cheese together until fluffy. Mix in the salmon with the dill and season with salt and pepper.

- Thickly spread the cheese mixture over 6 slices of rye bread. Place three spread slices on top of one another. Top with an unspread slice. Repeat with the rest of the bread so that you have two triple layers. Press down firmly. Wrap the layers in clingfilm and refrigerate for about 1 hour until firm.

- Take the layered bread out of the refrigerator. Slice each layer with a sharp knife into 8 squares and arrange on a serving dish.

Soups

Cauliflower Soup with Cheese Puffs

serves 4 | preparation: approx. 40 min | oven: 5 min

50 g butter
1 large potato, peeled and cubed
1 onion, finely chopped
1 litre / 2 pints vegetable stock
500 g / 1 lb cauliflower florets
50 ml / 2 fl oz. milk
30 g flour
1 egg, beaten
2 tablespoons grated mature cheese
100 ml / 3 ½ fl oz cream
pinch nutmeg
salt and freshly ground pepper
2 tablespoons finely chopped parsley

- In a large pan, heat half of the the butter and fry the potato and onion for 3 minutes. Add the stock and cauliflower florets and simmer 10-15 minutes.

- Make the puffs. Preheat the oven to 220°C / 430°F. In a saucepan, bring the milk and remaining butter slowly to the boil. When the butter has melted add all the flour at once. Stir until the mixture forms a ball of pastry and comes away from the sides of the pan. Take off the heat, cool and stir in the egg and cheese.

- Transfer the pastry to a pastry bag with a small, smooth nozzle. Squeeze onto a lightly greased or lined baking sheet, making small mounds about 1 inch apart. Bake the cheese puffs for 5-6 minutes in the oven until they have doubled in size and are golden brown.

- Puree the soup (save a few florets to garnish). Stir in the cream and season with nutmeg, salt and pepper.

- Ladle the soup into warmed deep bowls and garnish with the cheese puffs, cauliflower florets and parsley.

Dutch Pea Soup

serves 4-6 | preparation: approx 2 hours

400 g / 10 oz green split peas
½ celeriac , peeled and cubed
1 large carrot, peeled and diced
400 g / 14 oz pork chops
100 g / 3 ½ oz smoked bacon, cubed
200 g / 7 oz leeks, sliced
250 g / 8 oz cooked smoked pork sausage
½ bunch fresh celery leaves, chopped
½ bunch parsley, chopped
salt and freshly ground pepper

- Wash the split peas. In a large pan, bring 1½ litres / 3 pints water, the peas, celeriac, carrot, pork chops and bacon to the boil. Simmer for 1½ hours until the meat is tender. Add the leeks for the last 15 minutes of the cooking time.

- Slice the smoked sausage. Remove the chops from the soup and take the meat off the bones.

- Return the meat to the pan. Add the herbs, smoked sausage, salt and pepper to taste and simmer for 10 more minutes, stirring occasionally.

This soup is delicious with pumpernickel spread with coarse mustard and slices of smoked bacon.

Hearty Chicken Soup

serves 6-8 | preparation: approx. 2 hours | chilling: 2-3 hours

1 boiling chicken
1 onion, peeled and quartered
200 g sliced leek
1 large carrot, sliced
2 celery sticks , sliced
4 white peppercorns
pinch of mace
1 bouquet garni (2 sprigs thyme, 2 sprigs parsley, 1 bay leaf)
red pepper, cut in strips
4 spring onions, thinly sliced
50 g / 2 oz vermicelli
100 g / 3 ½ oz sweet corn (tin), drained
1 tablespoon finely chopped celery leaves
salt and freshly ground pepper

- Place the chicken in a large saucepan and cover with 1½ litre / 3 pints cold water. Bring the water to the boil and skim regularly to remove the foam that rises to the top.

- Add the vegetables, bouquet garni, peppercorns and mace and simmer for about 1½ hours.

- Remove the chicken from the stock and allow to cool slightly. Remove the meat from the bones and cut into small pieces. Strain the stock into a clean pan and season to taste. Allow the stock to cool for 2-3 hours and skim off any congealed fat.

- Heat the stock and add the chicken, red pepper, spring onions and vermicelli. Heat about 3 minutes on a low heat. Stir in the corn and chopped celery leaves. Adjust the seasoning.

Delicious with thinly sliced crêpes.

Brown Bean Soup

serves 4 | preparation: approx. 1 ¾ hours | soaking: 12 hours

- 350 g / 12 oz dried brown beans
- 2 large potatoes
- 2 bay leaves
- 6 peppercorns
- 3 cloves
- 50 g / 2 oz butter
- 3 onions, peeled and finely chopped
- ½ tablespoon curry powder
- 3 tablespoons finely chopped parsley
- salt and freshly ground pepper
- 2 tablespoons Worcestershire sauce

● Soak the beans 12 hours in 1½ litres / 3 pints lightly salted water.

● Peel and dice the potatoes. Add bay leaves, peppercorns and cloves to the beans and bring them to the boil in their soaking liquid. Simmer for about 1-1½ hours. Add the potatoes for the last 30 minutes of the cooking time.

● In a frying pan, heat the butter and fry the onion. Add the curry powder and fry a few minutes more.

● Remove the bay leaves, cloves and peppercorns from the pan. With a hand blender, puree the beans and potatoes in the cooking liquid. Stir in the onions and simmer the soup for another 10 minutes. Add the parsley and season with salt, pepper and Worcestershire sauce to taste.

Cream of Chicken Soup with Salmon

serves 4 | preparation: approx 25 min

1 litre / 2 pints chicken stock
30 g / 1 oz butter
30 g / 1 oz flour
freshly ground pepper
pinch nutmeg
few drops lemon juice
1 egg yolk
100 ml / 3 ½ fl oz cream
150 g / 5 oz smoked salmon, in pieces
2 tablespoons finely chopped dill

- In a saucepan, heat the chicken stock. In a large pan, melt the butter and stir in the flour and stirring, cook briefly. Stirring, pour in the stock and simmer gently for about 10 minutes.

- Season the soup with pepper, nutmeg and lemon juice to taste.

- Beat the egg yolk with the cream and stir in 5 tablespoons of the hot soup. Remove the pan from the heat and stir the egg mixture through the soup.

- Ladle the soup in deep plates or bowls and garnish with salmon and dill.

Cream of Tomato Soup

serves 4 | preparation: approx. 30 min

1 kg / 2 lb tomatoes
½ litre / 1 pint veal or chicken stock (ready-made)
2 onions, peeled and finely chopped
2 cloves garlic, peeled and finely chopped
2 tablespoons finely chopped thyme
125 ml / 4 fl oz crème fraîche
salt and freshly ground pepper
1 tablespoon finely chopped mixed fresh herbs

- Wash the tomatoes and halve them. In a large saucepan bring the stock, tomatoes, onion, garlic and thyme to the boil. Allow to simmer for 20 minutes.

- Puree the soup in a blender or with a hand blender and stir in the crème fraîche. Season to taste with salt, pepper and the fresh herbs.

Delicious with crispy cheese straws.

Asparagus Soup with Ham and Egg Mimosa

serves 4 | preparation: approx 45 min

300 g / 10 oz white asparagus
3/4 litre / 1 1/2 pints vegetable stock (ready-made)
1 teaspoon sugar
30 g / 1 oz butter
30 g / 1 oz flour
100 ml / 3 1/2 fl oz cream
pinch grated mace
salt and freshly ground pepper
200 g / 7 oz ham off the bone
3 eggs, hard-boiled
1 tablespoon finely chopped parsley

- Peel the asparagus with a potato peeler (starting just under the tip) and remove the tough ends (about 1 1/2 cm or 1/2 in). Remove the tips (about 3 cm / 1 in) and cook in a little vegetable stock for about 10 minutes until tender. Drain.

- In a saucepan, bring the stock and sugar to a boil. Cut the remaining asparagus into 3 cm / 1 in pieces and cook 15-20 minutes in the stock, or until tender. Puree the soup in a food processor or with a hand blender.

- In a large saucepan, melt the butter and stir in the flour. Cook gently for 2 minutes and gradually stir in the soup and cream. Bring slowly to the boil and simmer for about 3 minutes. Season to taste with salt, pepper and mace.

- Cut the ham into strips. Peel the eggs and press them through a sieve. Divide the ham and asparagus tips among four soup bowls. Ladle the soup into the bowls and garnish with egg mimosa and parsley. Serve immediately.

Mashed dishes (stamppotten) and other one-pan dishes

Hutspot: Carrot and Potato Mash

serves 4 | preparation: approx ½ hours | stewing: 2 hours

400 g / 14 oz marbled braising steak
75 g / 3 oz butter
4 onions, peeled, 2 sliced and 2 finely chopped
2 bay leaves
1 teaspoon dill seeds or 1 tablespoon fresh dill
salt and freshly ground pepper
750 g / 1 ½ lb floury potatoes, peeled and cut into pieces
750 g / 1 ½ lb carrots, peeled and sliced

- Cut the meat into cubes. In a large casserole, heat the butter. On high heat, brown the meat on all sides. Add the finely chopped onions and continue frying. Add a little water, the bay leaves, dill, salt and pepper and cover. Simmer for 2 hours until meat is tender.

- Cook the potatoes, carrots and sliced onions in a little salted water for about 25 minutes until tender.

- Drain the potatoes and vegetables and mash everything to a fine puree.

- Add the braised meat and some of the braising liquid to the vegetables and mix until a smooth thick 'stamppot'. Season to taste and serve the remaining braising liquid separately.

Hete bliksem: Apple and Potato Mash

serves 4 | preparation: approx 40 min

500 g / 1 lb sweet apples (Elstar)
500 g / 1 lb tangy apples (Cox Orange Pippin)
1 kg / 2 lb potatoes, peeled and cut into pieces
300 g smoked bacon, in one piece
25 g / 1 oz butter
300 g / 10 oz minced beef and pork
salt and freshly ground pepper
300 g / 10 oz chunk smoked bacon
50 ml / 2 fl oz milk
pinch ground cloves
pinch cinnamon

- Peel, core and chop the apples. Put the potatoes in a large saucepan and cover with water. Scatter the chopped apples over the potatoes and place the smoked bacon on top. Partially cover and cook about 25 minutes until tender.

- In a frying pan, heat the butter and stir-fry the mince until brown and tender. Season to taste.

- Drain the potatoes and apples and remove the bacon from the pan. Dice the bacon. In a saucepan, heat the milk with the cloves and cinnamon.

- Mash the potato and apple to a puree. Add just enough spiced milk to make a creamy mash. Add the mince and diced bacon and serve immediately.

White Bean and Carrot Stew

serves 4 | preparation: approx. 30 min | stewing: 1-1½ hours

2 large carrots
1 large pot white beans (700 g / 1 ½ lb), drained
50 g / 2 oz butter
600 g / 20 oz stewing beef, cubed
2 shallots, peeled and finely chopped
3 cloves garlic, peeled and finely chopped
salt and freshly ground pepper
200 ml / 7 fl oz beef stock (ready-made)
1 red pepper, cut into strips
1 teaspoon paprika
1 small tin tomato puree

- Peel and dice the carrots. Rinse the white beans under cold running water and drain in a sieve.

- In a casserole, heat the butter and brown the meat on all sides. Add the shallots and garlic and continue frying over a high heat. Season with salt and pepper. Pour in the stock and leave the meat to simmer on a low heat for 1-1½ hours until tender.

- Add the carrot, white beans, pepper, paprika and tomato puree to the meat and cook gently for a further 20 minutes. Add more stock if needed. Serve on a warmed platter.

Delicious with a crisp mixed salad with cherry tomatoes.

Dutch Shepherd's Pie

serves 4 | preparation: approx. 35 min | oven: 25 min

- 750 g / 1½ lb floury potatoes, peeled and cut into pieces
- 50 g / 2 oz butter + extra for greasing
- 500 g / 1lb minced beef
- 1 onion, peeled and finely chopped
- 200 ml / 7 fl oz beef stock
- 150 ml / 5 fl oz milk
- salt and freshly ground pepper
- ½ teaspoon nutmeg
- 2 teaspoons cornflour
- 1 teaspoon Provencal herbs
- 25 g / 1 oz fine, dry breadcrumbs
- 25 g / 1 oz mature Gouda cheese or another mature cheese, grated
- 15 g / ½ oz chilled butter

● Cook the potatoes for about 20 minutes in just enough water to cover.

● In a deep frying pan, heat half the butter and brown the mince. Add the onion and fry 5 minutes more. Add the stock and leave to simmer for about 10 minutes.

● Preheat the oven to 200°C / 400°F. Heat the milk in a saucepan. Drain the potatoes and mash with the milk and remaining butter. Season with salt, pepper and nutmeg.

● Mix the cornflour with a little water and, stirring, add the mixture to the mince. Season to taste with salt and Provencal herbs.

● Lightly grease an oven dish. Spread half the potato mash over the base of the oven dish. Spoon the mince over and top with the rest of the potato mash. Sprinkle with breadcrumbs and cheese and dot with butter. Bake the shepherd's pie in the oven for 25 minutes until the top is crisp and golden brown.

Sauerkraut 'Stamppot'

serves 4 | preparation: approx. 1 hour

600 g / 20 oz sauerkraut
1 kg / 3 lb floury potatoes, peeled and cut into pieces
1 bay leaf
50 g / 2 oz butter
2 onions, peeled and sliced
100 g / 3½ oz cubed lean smoked bacon
2 tablespoons flour
4 pork sausages

- Bring the sauerkraut and potatoes to the boil in just enough water to cover the bottom of the pan. Add a bay leaf and cook for 25-30 minutes until done.

- In a frying pan, heat half the butter and fry the onions on a low heat for 15 minutes until brown and crispy.
In another, dry frying pan fry the bacon until brown and crispy.

- Put the flour on a plate and roll the sausages through it. Heat the remaining butter in a casserole and fry the sausages until brown. Add a little water and braise the sausages 20 minutes until done.

- Drain the sauerkraut and save the cooking liquid. Mash the sauerkraut and potato together and stir in the fried onion, diced bacon and bacon fat.
More cooking liquid can be added to make the 'stamppot' smoother.
Adjust the seasoning if necessary.

- Remove the sausages from the liquid and reduce it over a high heat. Serve the sauerkraut with the sausages and sauce.

- Delicious with fried pineapple slices.

Curly Kale 'Stamppot'

serves 4 | preparation: approx. 35 min

1 ½ kg / 3 lb floury potatoes, peeled and cut into pieces
2 onions, peeled and chopped
600 g / 20 oz trimmed and cleaned curly kale, finely chopped
1 bay leaf
salt and freshly ground pepper
1 smoked sausage (350 g / 12 oz)
150 ml / 5 fl oz milk
25 g / 1 oz butter

- Put the potatoes, onions, curly kale and bay leaf with seasoning in a large pan. Add just enough water to cover the bottom of the pan and cook about 25 minutes on a low heat until cooked.

- Meanwhile simmer the sausage for about 25 minutes in water, or follow the directions on the package.
Remove the bay leaf from the pan, drain the vegetables and mash them finely.

- Heat the milk and butter and stir through the potato and curly kale mash until smooth. If necessary, season with salt and pepper. Slice the sausage and arrange over the 'stamppot'.

Delicious with coarse mustard, brown sauce and strips of crispy fried bacon.

Endive 'Stamppot' with Mushrooms and Cheese

serves 4 | preparation: approx. 50 min

1½ kg / 3 lb floury potatoes, peeled and cut into pieces
salt and freshly ground pepper
250 g / 8 oz mushrooms
50 g / 2 oz butter
200 g / 7 oz chunk smoked bacon, diced
150 ml / 6 fl oz milk
600 g / 20 oz finely sliced endive
nutmeg
200 g / 7 oz mature Dutch cumin cheese (or any full-flavoured cheese with cumin)

- Cook the potatoes 20-25 minutes in just enough water to cover. Clean and slice the mushrooms.

- Heat the butter in a frying pan and fry the bacon pieces. Add the mushrooms to the bacon and continue frying.

- In a saucepan, heat the milk. Drain the potatoes. Mash until smooth and add the hot milk. Mix the endive, bacon and mushroom mixture, pepper and nutmeg with the potato puree and warm through.

- Cut the cumin cheese into pieces and stir into the 'stamppot'. Serve the dish immediately.

Chickpeas with Apple Salad

serves 4 | preparation: approx 30 min

- 2 tins or pots chick peas
- 2 Bramley apples
- 50 ml / 2 fl oz apple juice
- 50 g / 2 oz raisins
- 25 g / 1 oz butter
- 200 g / 7 oz smoked bacon, diced
- 2 large onions, peeled and finely chopped
- pepper

• Drain the chickpeas and rinse under cold running water.

• Peel, core and roughly chop the apples. In a bowl mix with the apple juice and raisins. Leave to marinate.

• In a large pan, heat the butter and fry the diced bacon until crisp. Add the onion and continue frying for 10 minutes more.

• Mix the chickpeas with the bacon and onions and leave to heat through for about 10 minutes. Season to taste and serve with an apple salad.

Delicious with sauteed potatoes.

Spinach Casserole with Tomato and Minced Veal

serves 4 | preparation: approx. 10 min | oven: 25 min

4 beef tomatoes
25 g / 1oz butter + extra for greasing
500 g / 1 lb minced veal
2 red onions, peeled and sliced
1 tablespoon finely chopped rosemary
2 tablespoons tomato puree
1 kg / 2 lb spinach, washed and trimmed
salt
cayenne pepper
Mashed potatoes for 4 (see page 105)
100 g / 3 ½ oz fresh cream cheese
50 g / 2 oz white breadcrumbs

- Preheat the oven to 200°C / 400°F. Thickly slice the tomatoes.

- In a large frying pan, heat the butter and brown the minced veal. Add the onions, rosemary and tomato puree and sauté for a further 3 minutes. Stir in the spinach, a little at a time, and fry quickly over a high heat. Season to taste with salt and cayenne pepper.

- Grease a casserole with a little butter. Spread half the mashed potatoes over the bottom and cover with the veal mixture. Arrange the sliced tomatoes on top and cover with the remaining mashed potato.

- Top with an even layer of cream cheese and finish with the breadcrumbs. Bake in the oven for about 25 minutes until the top is crisp and golden brown.

Main courses

Pan-fried Cheese Slices with Spicy Apple Compote

serves 4 | preparation: approx. 30 min

3 firm apples
50 ml / 2 fl oz apple juice
2 spring onions, thinly sliced
2 tablespoons ginger jam
2 teaspoons hot chilli sauce
salt and freshly ground pepper
300 g / 10 oz mild Gouda or mild Cheddar cheese (flat piece)
2 eggs, lightly beaten
100 g / 3½ oz fine, dry breadcrumbs
50 g / 2 oz butter

- Peel, core and chop the apples finely. In a saucepan, bring the apple juice and chopped apple to the boil. Leave to cook for about 5 minutes until tender and the liquid has evaporated. Stir in the spring onion, ginger jam and chilli sauce.
Add salt and pepper to taste. Refrigerate the compote until ready to serve.

- Cut the cheese into 4 equal slices, about 2 cm / ¾ in thick. Put the eggs and breadcrumbs in deep plates. Roll the slices of cheese in the egg and then in the breadcrumbs. Repeat, pressing the breadcrumbs down firmly.

- In a frying pan, heat the butter and quickly sauté the sliced cheese over a high heat for about 4 minutes until golden brown, turning once. The cheese slices are done just before they start to become runny.

- Serve the cheese slices with spoonfuls of apple compote.

Delicious with small boiled new potatoes and a lamb's lettuce salad.

Cod Braised with Tomato, Lemon and Parsley

serves 4 | preparation: approx. 20 min

600 g / 20 oz thick cod fillet
salt and freshly ground pepper
1 lemon
75 g / 3 oz butter
3 spring onions or one small leek, thinly sliced
1 small bunch parsley, finely chopped
2 tomatoes, skinned, seeded and chopped

- Pat the cod dry with paper towel; cut into four equal fillets and season well. Cut four slices of lemon. Squeeze the juice from the remaining piece of lemon.

- In a deep frying pan, melt 50 g butter and add the cod fillets. Scatter the spring onions or leek and parsley over. Sprinkle the lemon juice over and arrange a slice of lemon and some chopped tomato on each fillet. Season well and dot the fish with the remaining butter.

- Cover the pan and braise the cod fillets 8 minutes on a low heat until done.

- Arrange the fillets with the herbs and lemon on four warmed plates. Reduce the liquid in the pan by cooking 2 minutes over a high heat. Pour over the fish.

Delicious with mange-tout and small new potatoes.

Steamed Mussels with Herb Sauce

serves 2 | preparation: approx. 25 min

2 kg / 4 lb mussels
50 g / 2 oz butter
2 small carrots, peeled and sliced
200 g sliced leek
1 clove garlic, thinly sliced
2 sprigs thyme
1 sprig parsley
For the herb sauce:
½ tablespoon cornflour
125 ml / 5 fl oz crème fraîche
½ small bunch chives, finely chopped
½ small bunch chervil, finely chopped
½ small bunch parsley, finely chopped
freshly ground pepper

- Scrub the mussels thoroughly under cold running water, discarding cracked mussels or open ones that do not close again when tapped against the work surface.

- In a large heavy pan, melt the butter. Add the mussels and scatter the carrot, leek, garlic, thyme and parsley over them. Bring to a boil on a high heat. Cook the mussels for about 8 minutes, or until all the shells have opened (shake the pan a few times during cooking).
Discard mussels that have not opened.

- Pile the mussels and vegetables into a deep preheated bowl and keep warm. In the same pan, reduce 200 ml / 4 fl oz of the cooking liquid by two thirds. Mix the cornflour with the crème fraîche and add to the mussel liquid, stirring continuously. Stir to a smooth sauce. Gently simmer the sauce for about 2 minutes and then stir in the finely chopped herbs. Season with pepper to taste.

- Spoon the hot herb sauce over the mussels or serve the sauce separately.

Fried Plaice with Almonds and Orange Sauce

serves 2 | preparation: approx. 20 min

50 g / 2 oz flour
2 plaice
salt and freshly ground pepper
1 teaspoon paprika
50 g / 2 oz butter
1 orange, juice squeezed out
75 ml (3 fl oz) medium dry sherry
50 g / 2 oz flaked almonds
1 tablespoon finely chopped chives

- Sprinkle the flour on a plate. Pat the plaice dry with paper towel. Rub the plaice with the salt, pepper and paprika and coat with the flour.

- In a large frying pan, heat the butter and fry the plaice over a medium heat for 8-10 minutes until golden brown and cooked. Turn the fish half way.

- Put the plaice on 2 warmed plates and cover with foil to keep warm. Mix the orange juice and sherry with the cooking juices in the pan and boil rapidly for 2 minutes until reduced.

- In a dry frying pan, toast the flaked almonds golden brown. Sprinkle them with the chives over the plaice.
Serve the orange sauce separately.

Delicious with saffron rice and fresh garden peas.

Creamy Fish Bake with Broccoli

serves 4 | preparation: approx 25 min | oven: 25 min

500 g / 1 lb broccoli florets
salt and freshly ground pepper
25 g / 1 oz butter
1 large red onion, peeled and sliced
1 yellow pepper, sliced
300 g / 10 oz cod fillet
300 g / 10 oz salmon fillet
grated rind and juice of 1 lemon
100 g / 4 oz cream cheese
100 ml / 4 fl oz single cream
½ tablespoon fresh thyme leaves
pinch nutmeg
100 g / 4 oz cooked mussels
100 g / 4 oz peeled Dutch shrimps or prawns
50 g / 2 oz mature Gouda cheese or other mature cheese, grated

- Preheat the oven to 200°C / 400°F. Blanch the broccoli 3 minutes in salted, boiling water. Drain in a colander.

- In a pan, melt the butter, add the onion and pepper and fry gently for about 5 minutes. Cut the cod and salmon fillet into 3 cm (1 in) pieces and sprinkle with lemon juice.

- In a large bowl, mix the cream cheese with the cream, thyme, nutmeg, salt, pepper, and grated lemon rind. Stir in the broccoli, cod, salmon, mussels, shrimps and onion and pepper mixture. Turn into a shallow baking dish. Sprinkle with the grated cheese and bake about 25 minutes in the oven until golden brown.

Delicious with mashed potatoes and a carrot and parsley salad.

Beef Rolls Stuffed with Mince, Bacon and Gherkins

serves 4 | preparation: approx 20 min | braising: 30-40 min

a little milk
1 slice old bread, crust removed
200 g / 7 oz minced beef and pork
salt and freshly ground pepper
nutmeg
4 slices of stewing beef or uncooked roast beef (total weight 400 g / 14 oz) pounded as thinly as possible
4 bacon rashers
4 small gherkins
50 ml / 2 fl oz beef stock
25 g / 1oz butter
100 ml / 3½ fl oz buttermilk

● In a shallow bowl, soak the bread in the milk. Combine the mince with the bread and add salt, pepper and nutmeg to taste.

● Spread the mince evenly over the slices of beef. Place a bacon rasher and a gherkin on the mince and roll up the slices. Secure with a toothpick.

● In a small pan, heat the stock.
In a large casserole, heat the butter and on a high heat quickly sear the beef rolls. Sprinkle with salt and pepper. Add the heated stock, cover and braise gently for about 30-40 minutes until tender.

● Take the beef rolls from the casserole and remove the toothpicks.
Stir the buttermilk into the braising juices and serve separately with the meat.

Delicious with potato puree, green beans and a cucumber salad.

Spicy Roast Chicken

serves 4 | preparation: approx 30 min | oven: 1-1¼ hours

1 lemon
1200 g / 2½ lb free-range chicken, at room temperature
salt and freshly ground pepper
4 springs fresh thyme
50 g / 2 oz butter
pinch chilli powder
1 tablespoon curry powder
100 ml / 4 fl oz white wine

- Preheat the oven to 200°C / 400°F. Slice half the lemon and squeeze the juice from the other half. Pat the chicken dry with paper towel. Sprinkle the cavity of the chicken with salt and pepper. Stuff the chicken with the lemon slices, thyme and half of the butter. Close the cavity with a couple of toothpicks.

- In a small pan, melt the remaining butter. Add the chilli powder, curry powder and salt and pepper to taste. Brush the chicken with the spicy butter and tie the legs together. Transfer the chicken to a roasting tin (on a rack).

- Roast the chicken 1-1¼ hours in the middle of the oven until golden brown and tender. Baste frequently with the cooking juices. Cover the chicken with foil if it becomes too brown. Take the chicken out of the oven and leave to rest for 5 minutes.

- Put the roasting tin on a high heat, stir in the lemon juice and wine and boil rapidly to reduce to a thin sauce.

Delicious with broccoli and pan-fried potatoes.

Rabbit with Mustard Cream Sauce

serves 4 | preparation: approx. 20 min | braising: 1 hour

4 rabbit quarters
60 g / 2-3 oz butter
salt and freshly ground pepper
2 tablespoons fine mustard
2 tablespoons coarse mustard
1 ½ tablespoons finely chopped thyme
400 ml / 14 fl oz white wine
150 ml / 5 fl oz cream

- Pat the rabbit quarters dry with paper towel. In a large casserole, heat the butter over a high heat and brown the rabbit on all sides . Remove from the pan, sprinkle with salt and pepper and brush the rabbit with the fine mustard.

- Stir the coarse mustard, thyme and white wine into the cooking fat and bring to the boil. Return the rabbit to the pan, cover, and cook gently on a low heat for about 1 hour until tender. Turn the rabbit frequently.

- Remove the rabbit from the pan, put on a warmed platter, cover with aluminium foil and keep warm. Pour the cream into the cooking juices and reduce the sauce over a high heat.
Adjust the seasoning if necessary.

- Pour the sauce over the rabbit.

Delicious with braised Savoy cabbage and steamed rice.

Jugged Hare

serves 4 | preparation: approx. 20 min | marinating: 8 hours | stewing: 2 hours

1 chilli pepper, finely sliced
1 onion, peeled and cut in wedges
3-4 cloves
2 tablespoons finely chopped thyme
salt and freshly ground pepper
1 tablespoon red wine vinegar
500 ml / 1 pint red wine
1 hare, cut in pieces (ask your butcher to do this)
75 g / 3 oz butter
100 g smoked bacon, cut into small pieces
3 tablespoons flour
1 small tin tomato puree
2 thick slices spice cake, cubed

- In a large bowl, combine the chilli, onion, cloves, thyme and 1 teaspoon salt. Add the vinegar, wine and the pieces of hare. Cover with cling film and marinate in the refrigerator for at least 8 hours. Take the meat out of the marinade, pat dry and strain the marinade.

- In a large casserole, heat the butter and brown a few hare pieces at a time over a high heat. Remove from the pan.

- Fry the bacon pieces for 3 minutes in the remaining fat, stir in the flour and tomato puree and fry the roux gently on a low heat for a few minutes. Gradually, stirring with a whisk, pour the strained marinade in the roux. Stirring continuously, bring to the boil to make a thick smooth sauce.

- Stir the spice cake into the sauce and add the hare. Cover and simmer 2 hours on a low heat until tender.

- Serve the meat on a warmed platter and serve the sauce separately.

Delicious with sprouts and potato puffs.

Braised Chicken with Tutti-Frutti

serves 4 | preparation: approx 30 min | soaking: 8 hours | braising: 40-45 min

250 g / 8 oz tutti-frutti (mixed dried fruit)
1 cinnamon stick
3 tablespoons flour
4 chicken legs
salt and freshly ground pepper
30 g / 1 oz butter
1 onion, peeled and finely chopped
100 g / 3 ½ oz bacon, cut in thin strips
¼ l / ½ pint vegetable stock
1 bay leaf
1 tablespoon fresh thyme or 1 teaspoon dried thyme
250 g / 8 oz mushrooms
grated rind of 1 lemon
1 sachet vanilla sugar

- In a large bowl of water, soak the tutti-frutti and cinnamon for 8 hours.

- Put the flour in a shallow bowl. Season the chicken with salt and pepper and then coat with the flour.

- In a large casserole, heat the butter and quickly brown the chicken over a high heat. Remove the legs. Sauté the onion and bacon in the chicken fat for about 3 minutes. Add the stock, bay leaf and thyme. Return the chicken to the pan. Cover and braise the chicken on a low heat for 40-45 minutes until tender, turning the legs occasionally.

- Clean and slice the mushrooms. Add to the chicken for the last 10 minutes of cooking time.

- Put the tutti-frutti with the soaking water and vanilla sugar in a small pan and simmer for 20 minutes.

- Serve the chicken on plates and serve the tutti-frutti separately.

Vegetables and side dishes

Sautéed Herbed Potatoes with Garlic Cream

serves 4 | preparation: approx. 25 min

1 kg / 2 lb waxy potatoes
40 g / 1 ½ oz butter
2 shallots, peeled and finely chopped
1 tablespoon finely chopped thyme
3 cloves garlic, peeled
150 ml / 5 fl oz crème fraîche
50 ml / 2 fl oz yogurt
salt and freshly ground pepper
pinch of paprika
1 tablespoon finely chopped parsley
1 tablespoon finely chopped chives

- Scrub the potatoes, Leave them unpeeled and cut into equal sized wedges. Cook for 7 minutes in just enough water to cover. Drain thoroughly.

- Heat the butter in a large pan until brown. Sauté the potatoes, shallots and thyme about 8 minutes over a high heat until golden brown and cooked.

- Press the cloves of garlic into a small bowl. Stir in the crème fraîche and yogurt and season to taste with plenty of salt, pepper and paprika.

- Add the chopped parsley and chives to the sauteed potatoes and adjust the seasoning. Serve with the garlic cream.

Delicious with braised cod.

Red Cabbage Salad

serves 4 | preparation: approx. 10 min | standing: 2 hours

400 g / 14 oz finely sliced red cabbage
1 onion, peeled and finely chopped
5 tablespoons sunflower oil
2 tablespoons mayonnaise
1 teaspoon mustard
1 teaspoon caraway seeds
2 tablespoons lemon juice
25 g / 1 oz shelled walnuts

- In a large salad bowl, mix the red cabbage with the onion.

- In a small bowl, mix the oil with the mayonnaise, mustard, caraway seeds and lemon juice. Mix the dressing with the cabbage. Let stand for at least 2 hours so that the cabbage can absorb the dressing.

- Garnish the salad with walnuts.

Old-Fashioned Mashed Potatoes

serves 4 | preparation: approx. 35 min

1 kg / 2 lb floury potatoes, peeled and cut in pieces
salt and freshly ground pepper
200 ml / 7 fl oz milk
50-75 g / 2-3 oz butter
finely chopped parsley, optional
nutmeg

- Cook the potatoes with a pinch salt for about 25 minutes in about 3 cm (1 1/2 in) water.

- In a saucepan, heat the milk and butter. Drain the potatoes and leave to steam dry. Finely mash the potatoes with a masher or press through a vegetable mill. Add the warm butter and milk and stir until smooth.

- Stir in the parsley if using and season to taste with salt, pepper and nutmeg.

Braised Red Cabbage with Cinnamon and Raisins

serves 4 | preparation: approx. 45 min

- 2 apples
- 50 g / 2 oz butter
- 1 onion, peeled and finely chopped
- 800 g / 1 ½ pound red cabbage, finely sliced
- 150 ml / 5 fl oz orange juice
- 2 tablespoons soft brown sugar
- 1 tablespoon cinnamon
- 2 cloves
- 2 bay leaves
- 100 g / 3 ½ oz raisins

● Peel, core and finely chop the apples.

● In a large casserole, melt half the butter and fry the onions and apples for about 4 minutes until soft. Stir in the red cabbage and orange juice. Add the sugar, cinnamon, cloves, bay leaves and raisins. Cover and braise on a low heat for 30 minutes, stirring occasionally, until the cabbage is cooked.

● Remove the cloves and bay leaves and stir in the remaining butter. Serve the cabbage in a warmed dish.

Desserts

Apples Under a Blanket

serves 4 | preparation: approx 20 min | oven: 30 min

4 small Cox Orange apples
50 g / 2 oz raisins
80 g / 3 oz sugar
1 teaspoon cinnamon
25 g / 1 oz butter + extra for greasing
40 g / 1 ½ oz custard powder
800 ml / 1 ½ pints milk

- Preheat the oven to 175°C / 375°F.

- Peel and core the apples with an apple corer. In a bowl, mix the raisins with 2 tablespoons of sugar and the cinnamon. Grease an oven dish with butter. Stand the apples beside one another and stuff the hollowed out centres with the raisin mixture. Top each apple with a knob of butter and bake for 30 minutes in the oven until done.

- In a bowl, blend the custard powder and remaining sugar with 100 ml /2 1/2 fl oz milk to a smooth paste.

- In a small pan, bring the remaining milk to the boil and, stirring continuously, add the custard paste. Keep stirring until the custard is thick and smooth.

- Take the apples out of the oven, pour the warm custard over, and serve hot.

Stewed Pears

serves 4 | preparation: approx. 15 min | stewing: 2½ hours

1 kg / 2 lb small stewing pears
3 cloves
1 piece of lemon rind
2 cinnamon sticks
50 g / 2 oz soft brown sugar
200 ml / 7 fl oz red wine
100 ml / 3½ fl oz blackcurrant liqueur
1 tablespoon potato flour or arrowroot flour
sprigs fresh mint

- Peel the pears with a vegetable peeler and leave them whole, with the stems intact.

- Stick the cloves into the lemon rind. Put the pears, lemon rind, cinnamon sticks and sugar in a large pan and add the red wine and liqueur. Add enough water to just cover the pears. Cover, bring to the boil and simmer $2^1/2$ hours until the pears are tender.

- Discard the lemon rind and cinnamon sticks. Lift the pears carefully out of the pan and arrange on an attractive platter.

- In a cup, combine the potato flour with a little pear juice and return to the pan. Stirring, bring to the boil.
Reduce the heat and simmer to a smooth, thick sauce. Pour the sauce over the stewed pears. Garnish with a sprig of mint and serve hot or cold.

Delicious with cinnamon ice cream and lightly beaten cream.

Rice Pudding with Brown Sugar

serves 4 | preparation: approx. 1 hour

1 vanilla pod
1 litre / 2 pints milk
150 g / 5 oz pudding rice
4 tablespoons soft brown sugar
40 g / 1 ½ butter
ground cinnamon

- Split the vanilla pod open lengthwise. In a heavy pan, bring the milk with the vanilla pod to the boil. Stir in the rice and, stirring continuously, return to the boil. Simmer the rice gently on a low heat, stirring frequently, for about 50 minutes.

- Take the vanilla pod out of the rice, scrape out the black seeds and stir them through the pudding.

- Spoon the hot rice into four dessert bowls and sprinkle with brown sugar. Top with a knob of butter and dust with cinnamon powder.

Delicious with apricot compote.

Semolina Pudding with Redcurrant Sauce

serves 4-6 | preparation: approx. 30 min | chilling: 1-2 hours

800 m / 1 1/2 pints milk
the rind of 1 lemon
80 g / 3 oz semolina
125 g / 4 oz sugar
1/4 litre / 1/2 pint redcurrant juice
1 cinnamon stick
1 tablespoon potato flour or arrowroot flour

- In a heavy saucepan, bring the milk and half the lemon rind to the boil. Simmer gently for 10 minutes.

- In a small bowl, combine the semolina with half of the sugar. Remove the lemon rind from the milk and stirring, add the semolina mixture. Keep stirring until the semolina thickens. Lower the heat and simmer gently for 8 minutes. Rinse a 1 litre / 2 pint pudding mould in cold water. Pour the semolina mixture into the mould, cool and then refrigerate for 1-2 hours until set.

- In a saucepan, bring the redcurrant juice, 100 m /3 1/2 fl oz water, cinnamon and remaining lemon rind to the boil. Lower the heat and simmer gently for 10 minutes, stirring occasionally. Discard the cinnamon stick and lemon rind. Add the remaining sugar and stir until dissolved. In a cup, mix the potato flour with 1 tablespoon of water until smooth. Stir into the hot sauce. Keep stirring until sauce is thoroughly blended. Cool.

Turn the semolina pudding out onto a dish and drizzle with a little redcurrant sauce. Serve the rest separately.

Cobbler's Cake

serves 6-8 | preparation: approx. 30 min | oven: 50-60 min

1 kg / 2 lb tart apples
1 packet of rusks
3 eggs
50 g / 2 oz butter + extra butter for greasing
100 g / 3½ oz sugar
2 teaspoons cinnamon
1 teaspoon ginger powder
pinch of ground cloves
125 g / 4 oz raisins
icing sugar

- Preheat the oven to 175°C / 375°F. Peel, core and slice the apples. In a saucepan, cook the apples with a little water to a thick purée. Crumble the rusks.

- Separate the eggs and, in a clean bowl, beat the whites to stiff peaks. Lightly grease a 24 cm / 8 in cake tin with butter.

- Mix the rusks, butter, sugar, cinnamon, ginger, cloves, raisins and egg yolks (beaten) with the apple purée. Gently fold in the egg whites and pour the mixture into the cake tin. Smooth the top.

- Bake the cake in the middle of the oven for 50-60 minutes until golden brown and cooked. Allow to cool and dust the cake liberally with icing sugar.

Delicious with chilled custard sauce, lightly whipped cream or ice cream.

Buttermilk Pudding

serves 4 | preparation: approx. 25 min | chilling: 3-4 hours

2 lemons
12 sheets gelatin
125 g / 4 oz sugar
500 ml / 1 pint buttermilk
½ tablespoon sunflower oil
125 ml / ¼ pint whipping cream
2 envelopes vanilla sugar
250 g / 8 oz strawberries, halved

- Scrub one of the lemons and cut off a piece of peel, about 5 cm / 2 in. Squeeze the juice of both the lemons in a bowl. In a large bowl of cold water, soak the gelatin until soft.

- In a pan, bring 100 ml /3½ fl oz of water and the lemon peel to the boil. Simmer gently for 10 minutes. Remove from the heat and discard the peel. Squeeze the water out of the gelatin and mix with the lemon water. Add the sugar and lemon juice and stir until the sugar is dissolved. Stirring continuously, add the buttermilk. Cool until partially set.

- Lightly oil a 1 litre / 2 pint, non-aluminium pudding mould and pour in the buttermilk mixture. Refrigerate for 3-4 hours until the pudding has set.

- Whip the cream with the vanilla sugar to stiff peaks.

- Carefully run a knife around the top edge of the pudding. Place a large plate on top of the mould and turn both so that the pudding slides out onto the dish.

- Decorate with strawberries and serve the vanilla cream separately.

Curd with Prunes

serves 4 | preparation: approx. 30 min | draining: 3-4 hours

2 litres / 3½ pints full fat yogurt
the grated zest and juice of 1 orange
250 ml / ½ pint red wine or tea
250 g / 8 oz presoaked stoned prunes
2 envelopes vanilla sugar
½ teaspoon mixed spice

- Place a colander on a bowl.
Wet a piece of muslin or clean tea towel and squeeze out thoroughly. Line the colander with the cloth and pour in the yogurt. Allow the yogurt to drain for 3-4 hours until thick and creamy.

- In a saucepan, bring the orange juice, grated zest, wine or tea, prunes, vanilla sugar and mixed spice to the boil.
On a low heat, simmer the mixture for 15-20 minutes, until the liquid has almost evaporated and the prunes are coated with a syrupy sauce. Allow the prunes to cool in the sauce.

- Divide the curd over 4 dessert bowls and spoon over the prunes and sauce.

Baked Rhubarb with Meringue

serves 4 | preparation: approx. 15 min | oven: 20-30 min

500 g / 1 lb rhubarb, sliced
75 ml / 3 fl oz red grape juice
1 tablespoon custard powder
sugar
2 egg whites
120 g / 4 oz icing sugar
½ teaspoon cornflour
½ teaspoon vinegar

● Preheat the oven to 175°C / 375°F. In a large saucepan, bring the rhubarb and grape juice to the boil. Simmer for 5-6 minutes until the rhubarb is tender and the liquid has evaporated.

● Remove from the heat and stir in the custard powder. Add sugar to taste. Transfer the rhubarb to a shallow baking dish.

● In a clean bowl, beat the egg whites to stiff peaks. Add a little icing sugar, the cornflour and vinegar and, gradually adding the rest of the icing sugar, whisk to a firm sticky mass. Continue whisking until the mixture is glossy.

● Mound peaks of egg white over the rhubarb and bake in the oven for 20-30 minutes until the meringue is set and golden. Serve immediately.

Index

appetizers, Herring in Mustard Cream 31
appetizers, Smoked Eel 31
Apple and Potato Mash, Hete bliksem: 59
apple Pie, Dutch 25
Apples under a Blanket 109
Asparagus Soup with Ham and Egg Mimosa 53

Baked Rhubarb with Meringue 123
Beef Rolls Stuffed with Mince, Bacon and Gherkins 87
Biscuit, Speculaas: Spiced 27
Bitterballen: Bite-Size Croquettes 35
Brabant Sausage Rolls 11
Braised Chicken with Tutti-Frutti 95
Braised Red Cabbage with Cinnamon and Raisins 105
Brown Bean Soup 47
Butter Cake with Apricot Filling 23
Buttermilk Pudding 119

cake with Apricot Filling, Butter 23
carrot and Potato Mash, Hutspot: 57
Cauliflower Soup with Cheese Puffs 41
cheese pancakes with herb butter, Poffertjes: Tiny 9
Cheese Puffs 33
cheese Slices with Spicy Apple Compote, Pan-fried 77
chicken Soup, Hearty 55
chicken with Tutti-Frutti, Braised 95
chicken, Spicy Roast 89
Chickpeas with Apple Salad 71
Cobbler's Cake 117
Cod Braised with Tomato, Lemon and Parsley 79
Cream of Chicken Soup with Salmon 49
Cream of Tomato Soup 51
Creamy Fish Baked with Broccoli 85
croquettes, Bitterballen: Bite-Size 35
Curd with Prunes 121
Curly Kale 'Stamppot' 67

Dutch Apple Pie 25
Dutch Pea Soup 43
Dutch Shepherd's Pie 63

eel Appetizers, Smoked 31
egg Salad, Tomatoes Stuffed with 17
Endive 'Stamppot' with Mushrooms and Cheese 69

fish Baked with Broccoli, Creamy 85
French Toast with Lemon, Wentelteefjes: 13
fried Eggs with Raw Ham and Mustard Cheese, Uitsmijter: 19
Fried Plaice with Almonds and Orange Sauce 83

Hare, Jugged 93
Hearty Chicken Soup 45
Herring in Mustard Cream Appetizers 31
Hete bliksem: Apple and Potato Mash 59
Hutspot: Carrot and Potato Mash 57

Jugged Hare 93

mussels with Herb Sauce, Steamed 81

Old-Fashioned Mashed Potatoes 103

Pan-fried Cheese Slices with Spicy Apple Compote 77
pea Soup, Dutch 43
pears, Stewed 111
Pie, Dutch Shepherd's 63
plaice with Almonds and Orange Sauce, Fried 83
Poffertjes: Tiny Cheese pancakes with herb butter 9
potatoes with Garlic Cream, Sautéed Herbed 99
potatoes, Old-Fashioned Mashed 103
pudding with Brown Sugar, Rice 113
pudding with Redcurrant Sauce, Semolina 115
Pudding, Buttermilk 119

Rabbit with Mustard Cream Sauce 91
Red Cabbage Salad 101
red Cabbage with Cinnamon and Raisins, Braised 105
rhubarb with Meringue, Baked 123
Rice Pudding with Brown Sugar 113

Sauerkraut 'Stamppot' 65
sausage Rolls, Brabant 11
Sautéed Herbed Potatoes with Garlic Cream 99
Semolina Pudding with Redcurrant Sauce 115
Smoked Eel Appetizers 31
soup with Cheese Puffs, Cauliflower 41
Soup with Ham and Egg Mimosa, Asparagus 53
soup with Salmon, Cream of Chicken 49
soup, Brown Bean 47
Soup, Cream of Tomato 51
soup, Dutch Pea 43
soup, Hearty Chicken 45
Speculaas: Spiced Biscuit 27
Spicy Roast Chicken 89
Spinach Casserole with Tomato and Minced Veal 73
'stamppot' with Mushrooms and Cheese, Endive 69
'stamppot', Curly Kale 67

Steamed Mussels with Herb Sauce 81
Stewed Pears 111

Three-in-a-Pan with Orange and Cinnamon Sugar 15

Uitsmijter: Fried Eggs with Raw Ham and Mustard Cheese 19

Wentelteefjes: French Toast with Lemon 13
White Bean and Carrot Stew 61

Zebras 37